Anagram of M

A Thriller

Seymour Matthews

Samuel French – London
New York – Sydney – Toronto – Hollywood

ANAGRAM OF MURDER

First presented at Southwold Theatre on 25th July, 1983 and subsequently at Frinton Theatre on 15th August, 1983, with the following cast of characters:

Augustus (Gus) Nation	Tony Scannell
Veronica (Ronnie), his wife	Nicola Davies
Sally Dure	Mary Bradley
Jeffrey	Nicholas Bailey
Detective Inspector Morgan	Colin Stepney
WPC Hughes	Juliet Brown

The play directed by Giles Watling

The action takes place in a study/drawing room of a large house in Frinton-on-Sea

Time—the present

ACT I

    Scene 1 A Saturday evening in early January. 6.30 p.m.

    Scene 2 Three hours later

ACT II

    Scene 1 A moment later

    Scene 2 The following day, Sunday, approximately 4.30 p.m.

ACT I

SCENE 1

The study-cum-drawing-room of a well-to-do house in Frinton-on-Sea. A Saturday evening in early January, 6.30 p.m.

The room is tastefully furnished in the older style. UC *is a doorway leading to the hall, cloakroom, downstairs toilet, kitchen, front door etc. The door is closed. To the left of the door, and slightly recessed, are some bookshelves with books, records and tapes on them. Beside the shelves is a hi-fi stack comprising record deck, tuner, amplifier and cassette player. To the left of this are the french windows leading to the garden area and back gate. Further left is a fireplace. Right of the door are more bookshelves and beyond a window looking out on to the drive. Essential furniture includes a large flat-top desk with drawers, on top of which is a table lamp, a telephone and an answering machine. There is a two-seater settee with a drinks table, behind it and a few upright chairs. Further dressing to reflect the taste of the owners should be added*

As the CURTAIN *rises the stage is in darkness. After a brief pause the following recorded dialogue is heard coming from the radio, but played on front of house speakers*

Male Voice You have ten more seconds to tell me where it is.

Female Voice I've already told you, I know nothing about the money; I had no idea he had any, and I certainly don't know where it is now.

Male Voice Such a pretty little face—even in the dark—shame to spoil it with a bullet-hole. (*Sound of a gun cocking*) Now c'mon, I need that money more than I need you alive.

Female Voice I swear I know nothing about it——

The gun fires; the girl screams

No please, please—I know nothing, I tell you, nothing at all.

A light comes on off-stage in the hall, discernible under the study door

Male Voice Dammit, somebody's coming. Now you keep quiet.

The door opens and Veronica, a beautiful woman in her early forties, enters and stands in the doorway, silhouetted against the light. The gun fires three more shots and the girl screams again. Veronica switches on the main light and goes to switch off the stereo tuner. Then she crosses to the drinks trolley and pours herself a drink whilst the Audience assimilates what has really happened. Then she goes to the doorway and shouts off

Veronica Gus, I wish you'd turn the radio off when you've finished in here! (*She saunters to the french windows*)

Gus enters and stands in the doorway. He is a professional writer in his early fifties, outwardly staid. He is wearing a dinner jacket and his shirt is unbuttoned at the top

Gus What's that? (*He crosses to the desk, takes a pack of cards from a drawer, switches on the desk lamp, sits and deals four hands for bridge*)

Veronica Every time I come in here I either get shot at by Afternoon Theatre or interrogated by Robin Day. I don't know which is worse.

Gus *Sir* Robin Day!

Veronica Oh, do I detect a note of jealousy in your voice?

Gus I would have thought it added a little excitement to your life.

Veronica What?

Gus My leaving the radio on, a little excitement, a little *je ne sais quoi*.

Veronica (*sotto voce*) Boy do I need it!

Gus Pardon?

Veronica Every little helps, of course.

Gus Now if you'd take up bridge, properly I mean, then you wouldn't have to stay at home on your own. You'd never get bored and you'd certainly never be lonely; it's a highly sociable game.

Veronica Nothing very sociable about saying "No bid" every ten minutes for hours on end!

Gus Now you're being facetious. Bid these for me, will you?

Veronica, with a sigh of resignation, picks up the hand to Gus's left. Gus will bid the hand he holds and the one to his right. Veronica will bid the hands to his left and opposite him. During the following dialogue Veronica quickly sorts out her first hand into suits and replaces face down on the table. She then picks up the hand opposite Gus, quickly sorts into suits, replaces face down on the table, picks up her glass and crosses to the drinks table to replenish it

Veronica I don't know why you don't get Sally to go through this little ritual for you, I'm sure she'd be only too willing to oblige.

Gus Now, you know as well as I do that our Sally has no card sense whatsoever, whereas you can be a demon player if you'd only relax and enjoy it occasionally.

There is a pause whilst Gus studies his first hand

(*Finally*) One club!

Veronica (*without a moment's hesitation*) One heart, five clubs!

Gus Darling, you know very well you can only bid one suit at a time, now don't play games!

Veronica Sorry. Having had *plenty* of time to study both hands, I simply bid to your left one heart; your partner five clubs.

Gus I beg your pardon?

Veronica (*with immense patience*) You, "darling", being the dealer, are presumably south; therefore west bids one heart, north *five* clubs; no doubt followed by resounding "No bids" from east, south and west, all three of whom are having a *highly sociable evening!*

Gus (*gently*) Veronica, you do realise what you need to make a bid like that, don't you? Especially after an intervening opening bid from your opponents.

Veronica (*facetiously*) Opponents! What opponents? I bid one heart as well, didn't I?

Gus Ronnie, when I open one *club* it does not necessarily mean I like clubs, it's a conventional bid——

Veronica Gus, just play the hand, will you? You might be pleasantly surprised. (*She starts to exit*)

Gus Lead a card, then!

Veronica does so from the hand to Gus's left

If I fail to make this contract it will be entirely your fault, I accept no responsibility . . .

Veronica (*kissing his forehead as she goes back to the doorway*) If you fail to make this contract, my darling, you should be court-martialled by the Bridge Club, buttons and epaulets flying.

Veronica exits

Gus plays the first two tricks won by east-west, then realises it is a lay-down five clubs

Gus Good God! (*He smiles*)

Veronica enters, carrying some TV magazines, glances at the cards on the desk in passing and sits on the sofa. A pause

You were right. Five clubs was made. Easily. I apologise.

Veronica No need.

Gus Sometimes I wonder if you have beginners luck or . . .

Veronica Or what?

Gus What will you do this evening?

Veronica There's a wonderfully gooey film on ITV.

Gus But you hate gooey films.

Veronica I didn't say I was going to watch it. I merely said it was on.

Gus All right!

Veronica (*over-enthusiastically*) I have a fantastic choice! (*She counts, indicating the choices on her fingers, occasionally consulting the magazines*) Gooey film, *Masterclass* on Two, er—(*She consults the magazine*) Rolf Harris on the didgeridoo, or *Shogun* on BBC One.

Gus What's that?

Veronica Oh come on darling, you know, that Japanese serial where they all call each other Napisan or something.

Gus You could go to Mrs König's cocktail party.

Veronica turns her head from Gus, closes her eyes, bites her lip

Veronica No, thank you.

Gus Why not? She's the only person I know who puts up with your awful practical jokes.

Veronica I do not play practical——

Gus What about the "Ugly Barley Water"?

Veronica That was just a bit of fun——

Gus One of many——

Veronica —so what?

Gus —at Mrs König's expense.

Veronica She asks for it.

Gus She particularly wants you to go.

Veronica And I particularly want her to go—*to hell.* (*Immediately*) I'm sorry, Gus, I know I promised not to insult your friends again, but that woman. I'm sorry!

A pause. Gus rises and crosses to the french windows and looks out

Gus May I borrow your car?

Veronica (*startled*) What? I'm sorry. (*Quieter*) What?

Gus May I borrow your car? It's raining, mine's in the garage for a service, remember?

Veronica Oh darling, I may want to go for a drive. Besides, you know how much you enjoy your walk along the beach.

Gus Yes I know. Normally I wouldn't miss it for the world, but if this is going to blow up into a force-niner, then I shan't want to know.

Veronica Oh, there's no chance of that, darling, it's barely a shower. I don't mind driving you there, but please leave me the car.

Gus Then how do I get home? Have you ever tried getting a taxi on a Saturday night, late, in this town?

Veronica Yes, I know.

Gus You could pick me up.

Veronica Darling, I might be in bed! Look, put on your big overcoat, take your brolly and brave the elements, you'll love it once you get started out, you know you will!

Gus (*managing a smile*) Yes, of course, you're quite right. There's something very bracing about a march along the promenade in this sort of weather, exhilarating. You know, knowing me I probably would've complained quite bitterly if it were a clear, still night, I'm very hard to please!

Veronica I had noticed.

Gus Mm, what?

Veronica I said mind how you go—darling!

Gus Oh good Lord, I'll be all right, nothing much can happen to me down there. Mind you, do you remember that chap, a couple of years ago? He was swept away, poor old fella—I'd forgotten all about him.

Veronica Yes, but he was much older than you, darling, wasn't he? A very frail old man, I seem to remember.

Gus I shouldn't think a force nine gale takes such things into consideration; great, solid oak trees have been known to succumb, and I'm hardly one of those!

Veronica Oh, I don't know. (*She smiles*)

Gus Flattery! On a Saturday night and *after* you've had your pocket money, too, what can this mean?

Veronica (*turning away from him*) I was merely trying to be pleasant.

Gus Of course, if something did happen to me you'd be left a very rich woman.

Veronica Gus, really . . .

Gus No, no, merely a statement of fact, it is true, isn't it? What would you do—in that event?

Veronica I have not the faintest idea, I've never considered it for one moment.

Gus Never?

Veronica Darling, you're a healthy, middle-aged man, as strong as an ox. When you're in your eighty-ninth year and in your dotage, *then* I might consider it.

Gus (*crossing to her; tenderly*) I could meet with an accident. Even solid oak trees have been known to succumb.

Veronica Not this oak tree!

Gus It could happen, an Act of God, the hand of fate, then all my little acorns would be yours.

There is a pause whilst Veronica looks at Gus

Veronica No, Gus. You're too lucky!

Gus sits next to Veronica

You're the luckiest man I know. You're the luckiest man I've ever known. "Accident", "accidental". They're not words in your vocabulary.

Gus It was "accidental" that I met you!

Veronica looks away

Well, wasn't it?

Veronica Yes, yes, Gus, of course it was.

Gus There you are then, an accidental meeting; my vocabulary has been duly blessed. Of course I know it wasn't an accident you were at the Tate Gallery, you used to go there all the time, still do, come to that, but me, I'd never been to the Tate before in my life. That's not to say I didn't enjoy it, the art, that is, I did, very much, and of course meeting you. Ronnie, I could cancel my bridge this evening, we could spend tonight alone, together, just the two of us. . . .

Veronica (*her eyes betraying alarm*) Gus, darling, we shall have endless nights alone together, but for me to come between you and your bridge, would lead to my certain excommunication from your circle of friends— all three of them.

Gus smiles, kisses her gently on the cheek, rises, crosses to the doorway and turns to her

Gus I'll tell you another thing, I'm the luckiest man *I* know, too.

Gus exits

There is a pause. Veronica stares straight ahead of her. Then she speaks, almost in a whisper

Veronica We shall see, Mr Nation, we shall see!

She breaks the stare, looks fleetingly about her, then rises to the window R to inspect the weather. She shields her eyes to see better, she can't tell if it is raining or not. She crosses quickly to the french windows, opens them, steps outside, hand outstretched to test the rain. She looks up and then about her. She smiles. There is a high wind, which we hear howling through the trees. She steps back inside closing the french windows behind her. Again she stares straight ahead

(*Almost whispering*) Perfect!

Her stare is broken by the mantelpiece clock chiming six forty-five. She crosses to it, checks her wrist watch, turns and crosses to the drinks table and pours herself a Scotch. She is about to replace the bottle on the tray, checks herself, then doubles the measure in her glass, replaces the bottle, adds soda from the syphon, and drinks heartily. She reacts with a slight gasp, the drink being stronger than expected

Gus enters and goes to the desk to collect a pen etc. He now sports a bow-tie

Gus By the way, darling, did you manage to flip through the notes of my new book?

Veronica Yes, yes I did.

Gus What did you think?

Veronica (*beginning to feel uncomfortable*) Looks fine, very promising, lots of interesting characters, situations, developments—though I did think the murder half-way through was a bit of a red herring.

Gus Yes, I think you're right; not so much the murder itself but the fact that it was so predictable. I mean, the way it builds up in the reader's mind, the bad relationship, she actually says she wants to murder him. Then when you get to the investigation, the inquiries, the questions—all the time the reader *knows* who did it. Signposts everywhere, boring, boring, and as you rightly say, a red herring, nothing to do with the main plot. Now red herrings are fine if they're used correctly, but they have to have a purpose. Now they can be a device for diverting the reader's attention, they can make him think something is going to happen which in fact doesn't happen. Or they can make him think something has happened which hasn't, he has to be led off in a certain direction away from the truth at the very moment that the truth is being revealed to him. Now I've had a better idea. . . .

Veronica replenishes her drink

I'll keep the same format, the same couple, he very rich, she hating him, then her lover appears on the scene, the build-up to a conspiracy between them, the plot to murder the husband for his money etcetera.

Veronica's eyes betray concern

And then at the *very* last moment, just when the reader is expecting the husband to be murdered the whole thing turns around and the husband murders the wife—perhaps the very day it was planned to happen, the very night, the very *hour* even. . . .

Gus stares ahead. There is a moment's pause. Veronica's eyes now betray alarm

Totally unexpected—by the reader that is.
Veronica And by the wife too, I should imagine
Gus What? Oh yes, yes, yes of course, naturally. Now, he makes it look like an accident in order to claim the insurance money on the policy he has taken out on her life. (*He is making this up as he goes along*) What do you think?
Veronica (*trying to shrug it off*) I'm afraid, I think it's a bit too—far fetched.

At some point during his speech, Gus finds himself above the table lamp on the desk. It shines up into his face, giving it an eerie demeanour

Gus No, no, not at all. Highly believable. I particularly like the murder switch happening on the very day, the very night, the very hour. (*An idea strikes him. He speaks slowly, deliberately*) Now wait a minute, the *husband* could kill the *wife* an hour or two *after she* thinks her *lover* has murdered *him*. Now that *would* be a surprise.
Veronica She would drop dead of the shock, I am sure.
Gus (*immediately*) What a great idea! (*He checks*) No, no, no, that wouldn't work.

The telephone rings. Gus ignores it staring straight ahead, reworking his plot. The phone continues to ring. After a while

Veronica Gus darling. The phone is ringing.
Gus Mm? Oh yes! (*He picks up the receiver*) Hello? . . . Mrs König, how are you? . . . Veronica? . . . Well . . .

Veronica gestures frantically that she does not want to speak to her

I'm not sure, I think you'd better speak to her yourself.

Gus holds out the phone for Veronica to take. He is clearly enjoying this. She reluctantly takes it

Gus exits

Veronica Mrs König! . . . Oh, Mrs König I was so looking forward to coming this evening, but I've got the most terrible bug . . . headache, sore throat, I ache from head to foot . . . the whole shebang. Yes, I know, such a shame . . . As soon as Gus has gone I'll take a couple of aspirin and go straight to bed, an early night . . . No, no, no please don't disturb him . . . it's not serious enough for a doctor, really . . .

Gus enters, wearing an overcoat and carrying a hat and umbrella

I might even treat myself to a brandy and hot milk before retiring . . . (*Her brow furrows*) An old sock? . . . Really? . . . (*She smiles distastefully*) Now what a quaint idea . . . Yes, I'm sure I shall . . . Goodnight Mrs König. (*She replaces the receiver*)

Gus Bye bye, darling!

Veronica I could kill you for that!

Gus Oh no, not tonight you won't.

Veronica (*looking suspicious*) Oh, and why not, pray?

Gus Because tomorrow is Sunday.

Veronica looks uneasy

> *Sally Dure enters. She is Gus's "girl Friday", a local girl in her thirties. She is carrying a shopping bag*

Sally Right, I've split them into two piles on the piano as you asked, sir, the originals on the left, carbon copies on the right. Was there anything else you wanted?

Gus No, no, Sally, that's all thank you.

Sally Shall I take the next lot, then?

Gus In the drawer, as usual.

During the following conversation, Sally goes to top right hand drawer of the desk, takes out a number of cardboard files, ties them together with some string and puts them in her shopping bag

Veronica (*still uneasy*) What did you mean, darling?

Gus Mm?

Veronica You said "not tonight, you won't, because tomorrow is Sunday".

Gus Did I?

Veronica What did you mean?

Gus Oh yes, well, Sunday morning I always bring you breakfast in bed and nothing, but nothing, could make you miss that!

Veronica But of course.

Sally Right then.

Gus Veronica and I have just been discussing the new novel, Sally—what do you think of it? So far?

Sally Oh, I hardly think I dare venture an opinion.

Gus Why not?

Sally Well, I don't really know much about these things. 'Sides I only type it out, I don't take much in when I'm typing.

Gus No comments?

Sally Oh, there was one thing.

Gus Yes?

Sally Well, the main character, the private detective chappie . . .

Gus The gumshoe, yes.

Sally (*not comprehending*) Well, I don't know about that, the thing is, I know he's a foreigner but you've given him a rather funny name, I thought.

Gus What? Willi Pap?

Sally That's it, Willi Pap!

Gus Oh well, that's that's only what his friends call him; his full name is Wilhelm Paprio; P. A. P. R. I. O.

Sally Oh Lor', I don't know which is worse. Doesn't sound very romantic for a hero.

Gus My dear Sally, I'm in the business of murky thrillers not Mills and Boon—but there is a reason for his name.

Sally Oh?

Gus You see, this new novel of mine is a sort of tribute to a certain genre of famous thrillers for which I have a great affection. Now the hero common to all these thrillers is also a private detective and Wilhelm Paprio is an anagram of his name—simple!

Veronica Oh Gus, really!

Sally Oh dear, not another one of your riddles is it, sir?

Gus No Sally, an anagram.

Sally Oh yes! What's a nanagram?

Gus It means, the same letters but in a different order, Sally.

Sally Oh yes, I know. George and I played that at Christmas, but you have to give each other clues, don't you?

Gus laughs

Veronica Well, Gus, give the lady a clue!

Gus (*consulting his watch*) I really must be going, I shall be late. (*He puts on his hat. To Veronica*) 'Bye darling. (*To Sally, taking her hand and kissing it*) "Farewell My Lovely"!

Sally Ooooh, I say!

Veronica (*forcing a smile*) Yes, this is turning into rather a "Long Good-bye".

Gus gives a nod to Veronica acknowledging she has solved the anagram

Sally (*seeing the clock*) Oh Lor', is that the time? I must fly, night all.

Sally grabs her shopping bag and exits

Gus and Veronica laugh together momentarily

Gus Goodnight darling, don't wait up for me.

Gus exits

Veronica Don't worry, I won't.

As Vernica crosses to the drinks table, we hear the front door shut. She pours herself a drink and crosses to the window R and parts the curtains. She waves a small wave

Sometimes that man can be infuriatingly attractive. (*She turns and looks at the phone on the desk*) But not for long. (*She crosses to the phone and dials a number*) Harry? It's me, are you alone? ... Good ... Yes, I know ... I'm sorry ... I promise never to ring you on this number again, all right? ... Don't forget ... After tonight I shan't need to ... Now listen,

everything is going precisely to plan, even the weather is *unbelievably*
perfect ... Jeffrey should be here in exactly two hours, and by midnight
Mr Augustus Nation—*will be well and truly dead.*

CURTAIN

SCENE 2

The same. Three hours later

*Veronica and Jeffery enter from the hall. Jeffrey is a handsome man in his
forties, but rather weak-willed. He is wearing evening dress and a sheepskin
coat with a large collar and is carrying a distinctive hat. He seems rather
unsure of himself*

Jeffrey It's quite a house.
Veronica Yes, I suppose it is.
Jeffrey Quite a town too, in its way.
Veronica You think so?
Jeffrey Well! (*He shrugs*) Of course, I've only seen it for one day, my day
  trip last month—a "recce" I think you called it.
Veronica I should imagine that would be enough to put you off for life!
Jeffrey Seems an OK sort of place, if you like that sort of thing.
Veronica *Like* that sort of thing? I hate that sort of thing; I loathe and detest
  that sort—oh I'm sorry it's just, this town. I don't know, there's nothing
  to do, nowhere to go. (*She manages a smile*) No-one to see. Oh Jeff,
  darling, I'm sorry, it's just that I'm so close to getting away from all this.
  I'm a little over-excited, that's all. You do understand, don't you?
Jeffrey Yes, of course I understand, Ronnie, but——
Veronica Oh, whatever am I thinking of, you must think me the worst
  possible hostess. Let me take your coat. (*She does so and places it on a
  chair* R *with his hat. Her sudden cheerfulness is very forced*)
Jeffrey Thanks. Ronnie, I ...
Veronica Now, how about a drink? Ah-ah, now don't tell me, every future
  wife should know what her future husband likes in the way of his
  favourite tipple. Shall we say bourbon on the rocks?
Jeffrey Right in one!
Veronica (*pouring a drink*) And don't think it strange that we keep
  American bourbon in the house, we keep a whole *range* of alcoholic
  potions, some of them quite lethal. (*This is a lie. The bourbon has been
  bought especially for Jeff to give him dutch courage, though she does not like
  to admit this*) Gus likes to entertain his friends in style, particularly his
  actor friends. You know, actors never seem to have more than one glass
  of the same drink, they mix them horrifically. I think they look upon it as
  the cheapest and quickest way of getting drunk.

*Jeff has now received his drink and Veronica pours one for herself. She
continues to babble nervously*

I remember one party we held here. Gus asked a certain lady what she would like to drink. "Something fruity but not too strong", she replied, so Gus toddled off to the kitchen to oblige. Now this certain lady just happened to be the town busybody—Mrs König's her name—and nobody's, but *nobody's* favourite person, so Gus mixed her one of his specials, a "kneetrembler" I think he calls it. I won't go into details but it was lethal stuff. So he offered it to her and said "This, my dear, is to the Ugli fruit what Ribena is to the blackcurrant". Ha! He called it "Ugli Barley Water". Well, I suppose in a way it did contain all three! Mrs König took to it like a red rag to a bull. She drank six before the evening was out, stayed sober as a judge—maddening! (*This story is true except it was Veronica who played the trick on Mrs König not Gus, who is teetotal. It is also* her *actor friends she is discussing*)

Jeffrey (*not terribly amused*) Sounds very funny.

Veronica Yes, it was rather.

Jeffrey I thought you said Gus had no sense of humour.

Veronica Oh yes, he has a sense of humour all right, a nasty sense of humour; anything that's at somebody else's expense, vicious sometimes. I remember ... (*She is here discussing her own sense of humour*)

Jeffrey Ronnie, don't, it'll only upset you. I know all about Gus' vicious side and I know what it does to you when you talk about it. I know what you've been through and I also know you can't take much more, but I have to be sure—quite sure—that there's no other way.

Veronica Jeff, please don't tell me you've had second thoughts about this, *please*. I couldn't bear it, I couldn't, if you let me down now. I need you, Jeff, I need you to do this one thing for me, don't you see? It's the only way we can be together ...

Jeffrey I'll not let you down, darling, I could never let you down, but don't you see; I have to be certain.

Veronica Jeffrey, ple-e-ase.

Jeffrey Ronnie, I've never killed before. I've never been a soldier, I've never been to war, I've never been involved in any violence of any kind. To kill a man I've never even met, is a *very difficult thing to do*. It's not something one undertakes lightly.

Veronica Oh, darling Jeff, don't you see? We made one mistake, many years ago, we've been given a second chance. Don't pass up this opportunity, please.

Jeffrey Ronnie, have you really, honestly asked yourself if it could be done some other way?

Veronica I've been over it in my mind thousands of times, I've been over it with *you* hundreds of times. Gus's family are Catholic, he'd never give me a divorce. You have no money of your own, I have no money of *my* own—not any more—we'd be penniless. All my life I've had money; here at my fingertips is more money than I've ever dreamt of. I couldn't live without it now, no way. If you love me ...

Jeffrey All right, all right, don't say it. If I love you, I'll do this to prove it.

Veronica I wasn't going to say that, darling!

Jeffrey You didn't have to; you sure as hell implied it.

Veronica (*slightly angry*) Jeffrey!

Jeffrey Don't, Ronnie, there's no need. I know damn well what I have to do, I've known for days. I just need reassuring, that's all, every hour on the hour. I guess I'm losing faith in my own judgement. I don't know ... what I do know is, the last eight years have been the most miserable of my life; letting you go was the most stupid thing I ever did, I should've fought harder to keep you.

Veronica (*moving to him*) I wish you had.

Jeffrey No, please, let me finish. I thought I'd drown my sorrows by throwing myself into my work. Off I went to America to become a successful screenwriter; disaster dogs my footsteps, and I fail at that, too. And then four weeks ago at the Tate Gallery, quite by chance, I run into you again. Since then I've been—reborn. I know that I love you more than anything else in my life, I know that I can't live without you ever again and I know I'll do whatever it takes to keep you. If that means—that I must kill your husband, then so be it!

Veronica (*in a whisper*) So be it.

Jeffrey So, I'm suitably reassured—for the next sixty minutes anyhow. (*He drinks heartily*)

Veronica Good, but you mustn't think of it like that, really you mustn't. You just ease him over the wall, into the water.

Jeffrey Having first knocked him unconscious.

Veronica Well, the sea will do the rest.

Jeffrey (*with a wry smile*) Murder by sea or seas unknown.

Veronica (*smiling*) That's right!

Jeffrey You know, I still can't believe my luck. I just don't believe it. A month ago I went to the Tate Gallery, more out of nostalgia than anything else. I simply wanted to wallow in the past for an hour or two. We always met on a Friday, so I go on a Friday; always at tea-time, so I go to the cafeteria. I order my coffee and gateau, I sit at the corner table. After a while I look up. (*He looks at her*) Where did you come from? I don't remember seeing any wings.

Veronica What?

Jeffrey My angel of mercy, come to save me from—what? What would I be doing? Where would I be? If I hadn't chanced upon you?

Veronica I don't know, my darling, but wherever it is, I'm awfully glad you're not there. Feeling better now?

Jeffrey Much!

Veronica Another drink?

Jeffrey Double!

Veronica gets him another drink

Now. (*He rubs his hands*) As they do in all the best movies, I suppose we'd better run over the plan one last time!

Veronica You first.

Jeffrey Well: my alibi is well-established. I went to the Embassy reception at six o'clock——

Veronica You managed to get an invitation OK, then?

Jeffrey No problem! The cultural attaché at Grosvenor Square was well impressed with my credentials—though why they chose to hold the party in the Barbican I can't imagine. The most difficult part of the evening was finding the way out! Anyway, I arrived at six and chatted up as many guests as I could; I'm sure at least half a dozen would remember me if asked. One especially, I think, would remember me, a little blonde from Milwaukee; I'm afraid I stayed chatting to her far longer than I should have . . .

Veronica (*playfully*) I see.

Jeffrey Oh, don't worry, you've no competition there. She had an accent you could cut with a knife, I had great difficulty in understanding what she was saying.

Veronica Oh, I'm sure you were too busy looking to be listening.

Jeffrey Well, maybe. Anyway, to make love to her, you'd need an interpreter I shouldn't wonder.

Veronica Aren't we wandering from the point, just a little?

Jeffrey Mm? Oh yes, sorry. Anyway, as I said I button-holed as many guests as I could and slipped away at seven-thirty.

Veronica Nobody saw you leave?

Jeffrey Nobody saw me leave! As far as they know I'm still there; as far as the world will know tomorrow, should they care, I left the reception at nine-thirty and drove straight to Harwich.

Veronica Good.

Jeffrey Ronnie, don't you think all this is getting a bit too "cloak and dagger"? I mean, is it really necessary? Why do I need an alibi, nobody's ever going to connect me with Gus.

Veronica I want everything to be perfect, I want nothing left to chance, every eventuality must be covered. If you and I set up home together when this is all over, then someone just might start to wonder where you were on the night in question. After all, my darling, this is going to be the perfect crime, you know.

Jeffrey *If* you and I set up home together?

Veronica *When!*

Jeffrey That's better.

Veronica Right. So, that's your alibi covered. Now what do you do from here on in?

Jeffrey What do I do from here on in? Well, first of all I hold out my empty glass to the lady on my right in the fervent hope that she'll refill it with another double bourbon.

Jeffrey holds out his glass. Veronica takes it but does not move

Veronica OK, what next?

Jeffrey What next?

Veronica Yes, what next?

Jeffrey thinks for a moment, then shrugs his shoulders

Jeffrey She does so!

Veronica smiles, amused by his playfulness, and takes his glass to refill it. She is quite happy to indulge him at the moment, as she is more than pleased with his change of mood. She hands him his drink

Veronica And then?

Jeffrey And then I sit quietly and relax, a large bourbon in one hand and a beautiful woman in the other. (*He drinks*) ·

Veronica looks at him questioningly; a look which says "and then?" without vocalising it

Yes, and then at ten forty-five p.m. precisely I get in my car and drive down to the, er, Greensward?

Veronica nods

I park at the bottom of Second Avenue, out of sight. I switch off the lights and walk casually across the Greensward, making sure there's nobody about. I walk across the Greensward and down to the lower wall. There I hide among the beach huts until a certain party comes along. This certain party will have finished his bridge evening at the, er—(*He looks at her*)

Veronica The Hartleys!

Jeffrey The Hartleys! He will have finished his bridge game at the Hartleys at precisely eleven p.m. This he does every Saturday evening throughout the winter and being a staunch creature of habit he will do so again this evening. (*He is by this time slightly drunk, which is why he is gently elaborating the plan*) As usual his route will take him also across the Greensward and down to the promenade, where at approximately eleven-thirty our paths should cross. He will be instantly recognizable to me because he will be wearing? . . . (*He looks at Veronica*)

Veronica A large black overcoat, black hat, and black umbrella.

Jeffrey (*facetiously*) Instantly recognizable in the dark, of course.

Veronica You will see enough.

Jeffrey (*smiling*) So, when our paths cross I shall then offer him an alternative route, namely, due east across the North Sea, a delightful stroll despite the weather! He will of course accept my invitation because of my irresistible charm, but should he show any signs of reluctance then a little gentle persuasion may have to be used. (*He raises his glass*)

Veronica Jeff, darling, don't you think you've had enough?

Jeffrey Then, having employed my diversionary tactics I return to my car and drive straight to Harwich and on to the night ferry to the Hook. Should I have time I will ring you with the code message from Harwich; if not I shall ring you from the Hook tomorrow morning before driving on to the Valpierre Hotel in Brussels.

Veronica You made sure, of course, that the U.S. Embassy people knew you'd be at the Valpierre tomorrow?

Jeffrey I should think by now the entire C.I.A. network knows it.

Veronica And the code message?

Jeffrey If all goes according to plan, I phone your number and ask for Mrs Stewart—S for successful. And if something went wrong, I ask for Mrs Unwin—U for unsuccessful. If you're not alone you say "No, sorry, wrong number" and hang up. In which case you phone me later in the day at the Valpierre. (*Sarcastically*) All frightfully 007 and all that!

Veronica You remembered everything.

Jeffrey I had a good teacher. Now, what about you?

Veronica What about me?

Jeffrey Well, *your* alibi, *your* plan of action.

Veronica I don't have an alibi, I don't need one. Jeff, darling, who could possibly believe that I could push a twelve stone man into the sea? As for my plan of action, after you've left I shall simply go straight to bed and presumably to sleep.

Jeffrey I've no doubt that you will, and very soundly too.

Veronica And in the morning, when I discover Gus is missing I shall phone the Hartleys, a few friends and eventually the Police!

Jeffrey After you've had the call from me.

Veronica Of course.

Jeffrey I need another drink! (*He crosses to the drinks table*)

Veronica Jeff, please.

Jeffrey Yes, you're right. I need to keep a clear head, don't I? What I *need* is a cup of black coffee. What a good idea! Now why didn't I think of that? Point me the way to the kitchen, I'll go and make some.

Veronica Sit down, relax, I'll make it.

Jeffrey Not on your life. I've never met a woman yet who could make a decent cup of coffee. Now, which direction is the kitchen?

Veronica Through the hall, past the front entrance, it's the door in front of you.

Jeffrey (*moving to the doorway*) Any for you?

Veronica No thanks.

Jeffrey Shan't be long.

Jeffrey exits

Veronica crosses to the desk and picks up the phone. She begins to dial and has just dialled the first digit

Jeffrey enters hurriedly

Veronica replaces the receiver

Ronnie! There's a woman coming up the path!

Veronica What?

Jeffrey A woman! She's coming here!

Veronica rushes to the window R and peers out

Veronica Oh my God, it's Sally!

Jeffrey Sally! Who's Sally?

Veronica Mm? Oh, she's Gus's secretary.

Jeffrey Well what is she doing here at this time of night?

Veronica How the hell should I know? Look, you wait here, I'll get rid of her. (*She goes to the doorway*)

A key, turning in a lock, is heard off stage

My God, she's got her own key!

Jeffrey Well, what do I do now?

Veronica Go behind those curtains, quickly! (*She indicates the french window curtains*)

Jeffrey hides behind the curtains

(*Calling off*) Who's there? Gus, is that you?

Sally (*off*) Oh, Mrs Nation. I'm most awfully sorry! I had no idea you were at home.

Sally enters wearing a long party dress with a coat over it and a scarf around her head

I thought you'd be at the party by now.

Veronica Er, no, I'm not going. I'm not feeling too well.

Sally Oh, I am sorry to hear that. If I'd known you were here I'd most surely have rung the bell. I hope I didn't startle you?

Veronica No, no—well, just a little. I had no idea you had your own key.

Sally Oh yes, Mr Gus gave it to me some weeks ago, in case I had to pick up any notes or returning something while the two of you were away. I thought Mr Gus had told you. I'm most awfully sorry, I didn't mean to frighten you!

Veronica No, no, that's all right. You didn't, not really.

Sally I'll return it if you wish.

Veronica No, you keep it, that's quite all right. But why exactly have you come back, Sally?

Sally Well, I seem to have mislaid one of Mr Gus's files.

Veronica Files! How do you mean?

Sally Well, you know that what Mr Gus writes in the course of one day he puts in a cardboard file with the day and date on it?

Veronica Yes, yes, I know that!

Sally Well, when I left here earlier this evening I took with me what I thought were the week's files to type up over the weekend, only when I got home I found I had Monday, Tuesday, Wednesday, Friday OK, but I didn't seem to have a file for Thursday.

Veronica Perhaps he didn't write anything on Thursday.

Sally Ah! In that case he always leaves an empty file, so as I know, see?

Veronica Well, perhaps you'd better check in the desk in case you left it behind.

Sally Right-oh.

Sally crosses to the desk and begins searching through the drawers. At some time during the following dialogue Veronica notices Jeff's hat and coat lying on the chair R. Veronica moves slowly across to the chair, carefully picks up the hat and coat and drops them behind the chair

Now, he always puts them in the top, right-hand drawer, but that's empty, so, it must be somewhere else. (*She searches other drawers*) But why he should put it in another drawer, I can't imagine. Ah! Here it is! Now that's why I missed it, you see, it was in the wrong drawer, should've been in the top, right-hand! Sorry about that, Mrs Nation, I won't disturb you any longer.

Veronica That's quite all right, Sally. Now let me show you out.

Sally Would you mind terribly if I went through your garden and out the back gate, it's so much quicker to Mrs König's that way. If I have to go round the block again, that wind will blow my permanent into a haystack, I know it will.

Veronica makes to object, but before she can do so Sally has drawn the french window curtain L and opens the door L

You get a good night's sleep now, Mrs Nation. I'm sure you'll feel better in the morning.

Sally exits through the french windows

Veronica is at once startled and relieved that Jeffrey was not discovered. A momentary pause, then she moves across to the french windows and takes a step outside

Veronica (*in a loud whisper*) Jeff, where are you?

Jeffrey pulls aside the french window curtain R behind which he has been standing, and emerges into the room

Jeffrey I'm in here, I think. I'm not altogether sure!

Veronica (*startled, she re-enters the room*) Jeff, darling, did she see you?

Jeffrey Not as far as I know. I certainly didn't see her.

Veronica Thank God.

Jeffrey She didn't sound like the cool, efficient secretary type, I must say.

Veronica Oh, she's more of an overblown typist. She types up Gus' notes, that's all. She's the only person who can understand them, he's known her for years, stupid woman.

Jeffrey She's a guest at Mrs König's too, is she?

Veronica Who, Sally? Good heavens, no! She serves the drinks and hands round the salt and vinegar flavour—manages to spill most of them, too.

Jeffrey Still, she didn't rumble us, so no harm done.

Veronica No, I suppose not.

Jeffrey What's your old man writing, that she was getting so excited about?

Veronica Oh, some novel or other, I don't really know. I don't take too much interest. (*She is uneasy at Jeffrey's question. The plot of Gus' novel is too close to reality for comfort*)

Jeffrey Well, he won't finish it now, will he?

Veronica registers this but does not answer

Funny we should both be writers, don't you think? Or is it that you have a "fatal" attraction to the breed? Mind you, he's been a damn sight more successful than I have.

Veronica You're forgetting; Gus's foray into Hollywood was even more disastrous than yours, my darling.

Jeffrey Oh yes, that's true.

Veronica Even *with* the help of his father!

Jeffrey Yes, of course. Alexander Nation, quite a director in his day.

Veronica Oh, I'll grant you that! But even more obnoxious than his son, if that's possible. His favourite party piece was to tell the world that when Gus's brother was born, D. W. Griffiths had just completed his finest movie, so the great D. W. honoured the Nation family by naming his new film after the great event.

Jeffrey Oh really?

Veronica *Birth of a Nation.*

Jeffrey Ha! Ha! I thought for a moment you were going to say *Intolerance.*

As they both begin to see the joke, they dissolve into laughter. This breaks the ice again between them

Veronica Oh Jeff darling, I do *so* wish you could have said that to the old man's face, I really do. It would have been a picture.

She laughs again. They find themselves closer together. They touch hands. She draws him closer still. They kiss tenderly.

Would you still like that cup of coffee?

Jeffrey No thanks. Suddenly I'm perfectly sober again.

Veronica I think I'll help myself to another drink.

They release each other. Veronica crosses to the drinks table. A pause

Jeffrey Could you tell me where the, er, smallest room is?

Veronica What?

Jeffrey The bathroom. I'd like to wash up a little.

Veronica Oh, you mean the loo! Why didn't you say so? It's the second door on your right. What did you call it? The smallest room?

Jeffrey Well, I don't know. I never know what to call it in this country any more. In America they call it a "comfort station". Well, I'm damned if I'm going to call it a "comfort station" over here, especially in Frinton-on-Sea. I'd get arrested.

Jeffrey starts to exit. As he reaches the doorway, the phone rings. He turns, they both look at each other, taken aback. Eventually Veronica lifts the receiver and speaks

Veronica Hello? (*With mock relief*) Caroline! ... darling, how lovely to hear from you, it's been so long ... (*She waves Jeffrey away, giving him a reassuring nod*)

Jeffrey exits

You must tell me all your news ...

There is a pause. Veronica strains her head a little to look through the doorway. We hear a door open and close in the hall. Veronica turns back to the phone

(*Sotto voce*) Harry! It's OK, he's out of the room ... Why the hell are you phoning me now? ... Sally? ... So you saw her come up to the house, so what? ... Darling there's nothing to worry about ... she did *not* see

Jeffrey . . . She got what she came for and left . . . I handled it beautifully, you'd've been proud of me . . . Oh, Harry, I know . . . I can't wait for us to be together again . . . But I'm glad in a way, you won't be there tomorrow, I don't think I could face it if you were . . . (*She laughs. Hears a noise from the hall*) He's coming back, I must go . . . 'Bye! . . . I love you! (*She replaces the receiver and goes to the drinks table*)

After a while Jeffrey appears. He is just rolling down the right sleeve of his shirt. His left sleeve is still rolled up and he is carrying his jacket

Jeffrey Gossiping all done? I thought you'd be on there for hours.
Veronica Oh, one of her children was crying, she had to go. I said I'd call back tomorrow.

Jeffrey smiles

Jeffrey (*with mock seriousness*) I'm afraid I've a confession to make.
Veronica Oh really?
Jeffrey A small matter of a minor indiscretion.
Veronica Tell me more.
Jeffrey You're bound to find out sooner or later, so I might as well tell you now. When I first arrived in L.A. I thought about nothing but you for weeks, I couldn't get you out of my mind. Then I met up with quite a few shady characters. Anyway, one night three of us went out and, we all got pretty drunk. We ended up in Chinatown.
Veronica Well, you're here to tell the tale, so it can't be that bad. Go on!
Jeffrey Well, I don't remember too much about it, something to do with a bet, I think, but we found ourselves in a tattoo parlour.
Veronica Oh no. (*She laughs*)
Jeffrey Oh yes. (*He laughs*) Now I *do* remember it was *me* having the tattoo. Anyway, I asked the man to print a name on my forearm; your name.
Veronica I'm flattered.
Jeffrey Yeah, well don't be, not till you've heard the rest of the story. Now apparently I told him your name, Veronica, and I also told him what I liked to call you, "Ronnie", R.O.N.N.I.E. Well, I don't quite know what happened, but I ended up with this. (*He shows her his left forearm*)
Veronica *Ronika!?*
Jeffrey Yes, I know, I didn't even notice it till the following day. I just paid him the fifty dollars and crawled out the door.
Veronica Yes, but. R.O.N.I.K.A., with a K, it's neither one nor the other.

Veronica is quite amused by this, as is Jeffrey

Jeffrey I know, I'm sorry darling. I just wanted you to know that it does actually refer to *you*, Scout's honour. I wasn't about to let you discover it on our wedding night, now was I?
Veronica I don't know that I should believe you, Mr Shady Screenwriter. I think this Ronika is some Chinese floosie you keep hidden away in your Bel Air apartment. No! Better still! You keep her stashed away in a hidden opium den in deepest Chinatown.

Jeffrey Ha! You must be out of your tree. I wouldn't set foot in that place again if you paid me!
Veronica What? Bel Air?
Jeffrey Chinatown!

Now they are both laughing. Jeffrey pulls her closer to him, but she stops him and pushes him gently away

Veronica There'll be plenty of time for that, my darling. Right now we have other things to do. (*She steps back from him, crosses to the french windows, opens them and steps out*)
Jeffrey Where are you going?
Veronica I just want to check the wind hasn't dropped. (*Pointedly*) We don't want to have to postpone again, now do we?

She steps out to garden and surveys the sky. Jeffrey crosses to the drinks table, and pours a measure of bourbon which he downs in one, hoping Veronica does not see. Then he crosses to the window R, pulls aside the curtain and looks out. Veronica returns

Veronica It's raining all right, but there's no more than a breeze; that's all we need!
Jeffrey Well, it must be pretty sheltered out the back there, 'cos out here it's bending over the trees. If anything the wind's got stronger.
Veronica Thank God for that! Just one more hour, please, just till Gus leaves the Hartleys!
Jeffrey What did you say he was wearing!
Veronica Who, Gus? Black overcoat, black hat and umbr——

Before she can finish Veronica catches Jeffrey's eyes. He is staring at her, mortified

You're joking!
Jeffrey I only wish I were!

Veronica rushes to the window R and looks out. She closes the curtain and turns to Jeffrey

Veronica *Why?* Why has he come home an hour early? He never does that!
Jeffrey Well, he has this time!
Veronica The lights! Turn off the lights!

She rushes to the doorway L and switches off the main light. The only lights remaining on are the hallway off C and the table lamp on the desk

Jeffrey No, don't, he'll see it go out.
Veronica So what? What's so unusual about a light going out?
Jeffrey Yes, but ...
Veronica Don't go to pieces on me now, Jeff, please, OK?
Jeffrey OK, I'm sorry.

They are by now either side of the doorway, Jeffrey R and Veronica L

Jeffrey What do we do now?

Veronica I'm thinking.
Jeffrey But he'll——
Veronica Jeff, I'm *thinking*. (*A pause*) We'll have to do it here!
Jeffrey What?
Veronica We'll have to do it here. Well, at least knock him unconscious, and then drive him down to the sea in your car. The rest should be easy.
Jeffrey How?
Veronica How what?!
Jeffrey How do we get him unconscious?
Veronica You, my darling, hit him with something *very* hard.
Jeffrey Ronnie . . .
Veronica Behind you on the shelf there's a statuette; pick it up.
Jeffrey But, Ronnie . . .
Veronica *Pick it up*, damn you!

As Jeffrey picks it up we hear a key in the outside door

Sh, he's coming in. (*She is half listening, half peering out into the hall*) Dammit, I can't see the front door from here.

We hear the front door close

Wait, I think he's . . .

Another door opens and closes

Yes, he must have gone into the cloakroom, to hang up his hat and coat. Now listen, if he comes in here, you know what to do, right?
Jeffrey OK.

The phone rings

Veronica Oh my God!
Jeffrey If he answers that, we're sunk. You answer it, quick!
Veronica Are you mad? Let it ring!
Jeffrey But . . .
Veronica *Let it ring!* Let him come and answer it, only hit him before he lifts the receiver, OK? *Jeffrey!!*
Jeffrey Yeah, yeah, sure.

There is a pause. Jeffrey is to R of the door; Veronica to L of door. The phone continues to ring

Eventually Gus enters and goes towards the desk

Jeffrey comes forward; Veronica following. Gus picks up the receiver in his left hand and starts to raise it to his ear. Jeffrey strikes him from behind with the statuette and simultaneously Veronica grabs the receiver in one hand and clasps her other hand over the mouthpiece. Gus sees neither of them, but falls slowly across the desk, his arms above his head. This causes Veronica to step sharply to her left so that she is standing with her face immediately above the table lamp, which is of course still on. Jeff's gaze moves from Gus to the statuette in his hand; Veronica's gaze moves from Gus to out front. She removes her hand from the mouthpiece

Veronica (*into the telephone*) Hello ... why, Mrs König, how nice of you to call ...

As she speaks the last line Gus's right hand, fingers crooked, rises very slowly from the desk and reaches for the telephone wire

CURTAIN

ACT II

SCENE 1

The same. A moment later

Veronica Yes Mrs König ... I'm fine thank you ... (*She sees Gus's raised hand; she covers the mouthpiece*) Jeff! Quickly!

Jeffrey looks up and drags Gus off the desk on to the floor. As he does this he hits Gus a second time

Noise, what noise? ... Oh that, the phone slipped out of my hand ... Well that's very kind of you Mrs König, but I'm perfectly all right ... No, I just thought I'd stay up a little longer and watch the late-night movie on television; it's such a good film, I'd love to see it again ... What's it called? ... Oh well ...

She looks frantically around her and then notices the TV magazines on the sofa where she had left them earlier. She snaps her fingers at Jeffrey

It's got that lovely actor in it ... oh dear what's his name?

Jeffrey finally passes her the magazines

(*Flipping over a page or two*) Isn't it funny how you have a name on the tip of your tongue, yet you just can't remember it ... (*At last she finds the right page*) It's called *Murder Most Foul* ... (*She looks at Jeffrey horrified*) Yes it is good, isn't it? ... Er ... (*She consults the magazine again*) Er, Ray Milland ... Did you really? ... How nice for you, that must have been fun ... Mrs König, I really ... Yes, didn't he just ... Such a pity ... You are most awfully kind ... Thank you so much ... Goodnight Mrs König ... (*She replaces the receiver*) Interfering bitch!

Jeffrey and Veronica give each other a long look; then they survey Gus who is prostrate on the floor

Jeffrey Well? (*A pause*) Well?
Veronica It's quite simple, we put him in the boot of your car, drive him down to the beach and—drop him into the sea. OK?
Jeffrey OK.

A pause

Veronica Well?
Jeffrey Yes.

Jeffrey notices the statuette in his hand, looks around not knowing where to put

*it, and eventually places it on the desk. He then picks up Gus under the arms
and drags him to the doorway. He stops*

Hey, wait a minute, my car's a quarter of a mile away. I can't carry him all
the way up there!

Veronica (*with great patience*) Jeffrey, leave him by the porch, go and fetch
your car and bring it back here.

He starts to move

But make sure there's nobody about, OK?

Jeffrey exits, dragging Gus with him

*Veronica watches them go, then turns into the room. She closes her eyes and
takes a deep breath. She then looks about her, deciding what she must do. She
picks up Jeffrey's glass and the statuette; she then notices the items which have
fallen from the desk, if indeed this has happened. She replaces them and tidies
the desk. She crosses* R *and picks up Jeffrey's hat and coat*

    *Again she picks up the glass and statuette and exits to the kitchen,
supposedly to clean them*

A pause

    *Eventually the french windows open, the curtains part, and Sally creeps in
carrying a cardboard file*

Sally (*sotto voce*) Coo-ee! Mrs Nation! (*She places the file on the desk. She
makes to open a drawer and then stops. She looks across to the drinks table,
then the doorway, then back to the drinks table. She then creeps across to
the drinks table, pours herself a sherry, sips it, and tiptoes back to the desk.
She takes another sip, places the glass on the desk and continues to look
through the drawers*)

    Suddenly Veronica enters carrying only the statuette

Veronica Ohh!!

Sally Oh, Mrs Nation, I'm most awfully sorry. Oh dear, I've done it again! I
thought you'd gone to bed, you said you were going to!

Veronica Sally, what on earth are you doing here?

Sally Well, it's like this you see, Mrs Nation. That file I came for earlier, the
Thursday one ...

Veronica Yes, yes.

Sally Well, I took the wrong one, I've already done this one, I typed it out a
couple of weeks back.

Veronica I see.

Sally So I've brought it back, see. I only recognized it because I dropped
some of the files on Mrs König's kitchen floor. (*She giggles*) And while I
was picking up the papers I noticed several sheets with this thick red line
across 'em, you see, and I thought aye aye, 'e's been at it again, I thought.
Well then I started reading 'em and I realized——

Veronica Yes, yes Sally, but why bring it back now?

Sally Well, I've come to get the *right* one, y'see.

Veronica But why tonight, couldn't it wait till Monday?

Sally Well normally it could, but I wanted to get it all done on Sunday so's I'd have the week-days clear, see.

Veronica Well, I'm sorry Sally——

Sally It must be on the piano in the sitting-room along with all the others. If I could just have a look ...

Sally attempts to pass Veronica in the doorway

Veronica No!!

Sally is taken aback

I'm sorry Sally, but not tonight, anyway. That's right, I've just remembered, Gus was saying earlier, he's going to rewrite that section—er, the part where the actual murder takes place, that's it. Something about changing over the identities of the murderer and the victim!

Sally Oh, I see! (*She doesn't*)

Veronica That must have been what he wrote on Thursday, that's why he held it back. Well, it'll take him at least three or four days to rewrite it, so your week will be perfectly clear!

Sally Thank you very much.

Veronica So you just run along and type out what you've got, and that will be absolutely fine!

Sally Yes, right-ho, Mrs Nation.

Veronica Are you feeling all right, Sally?

Sally Yes.

Veronica Well, what is it?

Sally I was just wondering, why you were holding—that! (*She points to the statuette*)

Veronica Oh, this! Ha! Well, when I heard a noise in here it was the first thing that came to hand. I thought you were—a burglar!

Sally Oh, I see. (*She doesn't, but then suddenly realizes*) Oooooh! You mean you were going to hit me over the head with that, Mrs Nation?!!

Veronica Only if you were a burglar, Sally, and as it turns out, you're not, are you?

Sally Ooooh! No-ooo-o. I think in future I'll go to the front door and ring the bell, it's much safer! Sorry to have troubled you.

Sally dashes out the way she came

Veronica breathes a sigh of relief and then returns the statuette to the bookshelf. She then crosses to the window R *and looks out; then she crosses back to the french windows, closes them, draws the curtains and returns to the desk. She notices the sherry glass; puzzled, she picks it up, sniffs it and then looks toward the french windows. With a sigh of resignation she puts the glass down again. She picks up the phone and dials a number. There is a long wait*

Veronica (*eventually*) Harry? (*She quickly puts her hand over the mouthpiece, then slowly lowers the receiver and replaces it*) Damn!!

We hear the sound of a car, and headlights slowly appear through the window R. *The car stops with the headlights shining straight into the room. The engine is turned off and the headlights go out.* Veronica *takes an envelope from the desk and writes her name and address on it; from a drawer she takes a stamp and sticks it on the envelope; from another drawer she takes a key*

Jeffrey enters

Jeffrey Ronnie, look, I've been thinking. If I take him down in the car, I'll have to carry him across that Greensward down to the lower wall; now that's a hundred yards at least, you said so yourself . . .

Veronica That's OK, I've thought of that. You drive down Fourth Avenue—not Second, Fourth. When you reach the Greensward you'll see a gate—this is the key. (*She gives it to him*) Now it's late, so there won't be anyone about. On your left you'll see the Grand Hotel, on your right, two other hotels, but the bars will be closed by now, they're dead this time of year, anyway. Now beyond the gate is a short track down to a slipway, once you're there, you'll be able to "do whatever you have to" completely out of sight. Oh, and turn your lights off once you're through the gate, just to be safe. When you've finished come back the same way and make *sure* you lock the gate behind you; and whatever you do, under *no* circumstances bring the key back here, you post it to me in this envelope. (*She gives it to him*) Is that clear?

Jeffrey Very clear. You think of everything, don't you?

Veronica I try to!

Jeffrey Very efficient lady. Highly commendable in any normal situation, but when it's a woman plotting the murder of her own husband, somehow it's—oh, I don't know.

Veronica Somehow it's very necessary if you and I are going to get away with this.

Jeffrey Yes.

Veronica Have you taken him out?

Jeffrey He's in the boot of the car.

Veronica Don't forget his hat and coat!

Jeffrey Oh, I'm ahead of you there, I've got his coat and his umbrella.

Veronica Don't forget the hat!

Jeffrey Which hat? There's half a dozen.

Veronica The one that's wet, of course!

Jeffrey Ah! But he had the umbrella up, remember, it wouldn't *be* wet. (*He is pleased with himself at having thought of something that actually slipped Veronica's mind*)

Veronica (*smiling*) In that case, it doesn't really matter which hat, does it?

Jeffrey I guess not.

Veronica Come on, I'll get it for you, any black one will do.

Veronica exits followed by Jeffrey

(*Off*) You get in the car, I won't be a minute.

We hear the front door open, then a car door open and shut. Then the engine starts; the headlights come on and again shine through the window R directly across the stage. After a while the phone begins to ring. It continues to ring and eventually the car moves off, as do the headlights. We hear the front door close

Veronica enters slowly and crosses to the desk

She is undecided as to whether to answer the phone. Eventually she picks up the receiver and slowly raises it to her ear

Frinton double four, fo—— (*A pause*) Frinton double four, four three . . . Harry! . . . Darling! . . . I tried to ring you but . . . Yes, I know, but this is an emergency . . . Well the damn woman shouldn't have been in your office! How was I to know she was going to answer the phone . . . Look, Harry, will you be quiet for a moment and listen. Gus came back to the house! . . . Not ten minutes ago, but don't worry, everything's been taken care of, Jeff knocked him out and he's taken him down in his own car . . . Now don't worry, there's nothing at all to link either of us with Gus's death . . . *Everything is going to be all right!*

CURTAIN

SCENE 2

The same. The following day. 4.30 p.m.

It is dusk, almost dark. There are no lights on in the house. All the curtains are open

A figure appears silhouetted in the doorway. It is Gus, but he is wearing Jeffrey's distinctive hat and coat to conceal his identity from the Audience. The collar of the coat is turned up so his face is hidden. He crosses to the desk. A car is heard approaching the house. The figure crosses to the window R and looks out with his back to the audience. He then immediately crosses to the french windows, pulls the curtains closed and hides behind them. Headlights are seen approaching through the window R. The car stops with the headlights shining through the window. The engine is switched off and the headlights are extinguished. A car door opens and closes and then the front door opens and closes. The hall light goes on

Veronica enters, goes to the desk, and switches on the table lamp

She then closes the curtains at the window R and goes to the french windows to do the same. She sees the curtains are already closed. She shrugs this off, switches on the telephone answering machine and pours herself a drink. A few appropriate noises are heard from the machine before the messages are heard

Voice 1 Oh, er, hullo Gus, it's Jack here. I wanted a quick word about that old pot-boiler of yours; I'm thinking of putting it on as part of the Summer Season this year. You know the one I mean . . . I forget the title for the moment—*Cyanide Serenade*, I think it was. Well, if it wasn't, it should've been, ha! ha! Anyway, give us a buzz sometime, will you? Bye!

The machine utters more noises. Veronica paces up and down, restless

Voice 2 Oh, Veronica, do forgive me, I'm in a terrible rush. It's Daphne. We're having a cheese and wine on the twenty-ninth, fund-raising for the Friends of Frinton Theatre. Do let me know if you can make it, we'd *love* you to come. 'Bye for now!

Veronica Come on, Jeffrey, come on, *please*!

Voice 3 Er, Mrs Nation, it's Sergeant Webb here from the Police Station. I've been trying to contact you all afternoon, ma'am. We need to ask you a few questions about your husband's disappearance. Could you please telephone us as soon as you arrive home. Thank you so much. Sorry to have bothered you . . .

The tape runs on in silence

Veronica (*approaching the machine*) For God's sake, Jeffrey, where are you?!

The tape runs on some more in silence. Eventually she switches it off. She thinks for a moment, highly agitated. She then picks up the phone and dials. The phone rings for some time

Come on, come on.

Eventually it is answered at the other end. She puts her hand over the mouthpiece and listens intently. After a moment it is obvious it is not the person she expected. She slowly replaces the receiver

Oh Harry, Harry! I need you, what do I *do*?

She picks up the phone again and is about to dial when a car is heard approaching the house. She replaces the phone and rushes to the window R to see who it is. Headlights shine into the room as she opens the curtains

Oh damn! That's all I need!

She pulls herself together and exits

"Jeffrey" appears from the french windows, crosses to window R and looks out, again with his back to the audience. The light is dim; only the table lamp is on. We still cannot see his face. We hear voices outside. He crosses to the hi-fi stack L of the main door, flicks a switch, etc. and returns to behind the french window curtains

Veronica enters followed by Detective Inspector Morgan and Woman Police Constable Hughes. He is dressed in plain clothes, she is in uniform

Veronica switches on the main room-light

Do come in, won't you? (*She is highly nervous*)

Morgan Thank you, Mrs Nation. Just a few questions I should like to ask you. We shan't keep you long. This is WPC Hughes, she will be taking notes, if that's all right with you? I should point out that Constable Hughes is already aware of the fact that you and I know each other socially, Mrs Nation; and I shall continue to call you Mrs Nation if you don't mind er ma'am, as I'm here in an official capacity. Normally, of course, I wouldn't have been sent on an errand such as this, but we're very short-handed at the moment. Last night's storm caused a lot of damage around the town and all police leave has been cancelled, that's why I'm here. There's also a fishing boat reported missing with two men aboard and every available man is out looking for them, and looking for your husband, too, of course, Mrs Nation.

Veronica Do sit down, er . . .

Morgan Just call me Inspector, ma'am.

Veronica Inspector!

Morgan Thank you. (*He sits on the sofa* R) Would you care to sit down yourself?

Veronica No, thank you!

A pause

Morgan Well now, when did you last see your husband, Mrs Nation?

Veronica Yesterday evening, about seven o'clock.

Morgan I gather he went out for the evening. Could you tell me where?

Veronica To the Hartleys, to play bridge, as he does almost every Saturday. But then I believe you're already aware of that fact, Inspector.

Morgan Yes, quite.

Veronica Look, Inspector, I've already given these facts to the Sergeant this morning, is it really necessary to go over them again?

Morgan Forgive me, Mrs Nation, but that was on the telephone. We do need to get these things down in writing from the person concerned. And it's quite possible that in going over them again some relevant information may emerge which was missed the first time around.

Veronica Yes, of course. I'm sorry.

A pause

Morgan What was he wearing, Mrs Nation?

Veronica Er, evening dress—DJ, black tie . . .

Morgan Any raincoat or such like?

Veronica A black overcoat and hat.

Morgan What type of hat?

Veronica A trilby, I think!

Morgan You think?

Veronica He has several, they all look the same to me.

Morgan I see. Was he carrying anything? A briefcase, or such like?

Veronica No. Oh, er, an umbrella, he was carrying an umbrella.

Morgan Fine! And he was on foot, I believe?

Veronica Yes.

Morgan He didn't take the car?

Veronica No, Inspector, he always walked to the Hartleys, along the sea front. He was—is—very fond of walking, my husband. But then I believe you're well aware of that fact too, Inspector!

Morgan Quite, and he always walked back the same way?

Veronica Always!

Morgan Thank you, Mrs Nation. If there's any other information which
you think might help us ...?

Hughes There is one thing, sir, if I might?

Morgan looks disapprovingly at the constable

Mrs Nation, we have been trying to contact you most of the day since you
reported your husband missing, would you mind telling us where you've
been?

Veronica (*indignantly*) Looking for my husband, of course!

Hughes Yes, but ...

Morgan (*conciliatory*) I think, what the constable means, Mrs Nation, is
that our men have been searching the beach area all day, yet no-one
appears to have seen you there.

Veronica I drove inland, I don't know why, I just wanted to get away—
sitting here all alone, waiting, not knowing what had happened to Gus. I
had to do something, to get out. I, I, I drove to the estuary over by Kirby-
le-Soken. Gus often used to walk there, it was one of his favourite spots. I
just thought, maybe ... I walked for miles, but there was no sign.

Morgan Of course, Mrs Nation, please accept my apologies. (*He again
looks disapprovingly at the constable*) I'm sure the constable didn't mean
to upset you. She was only trying to do her job.

Veronica That's quite all right.

Morgan Would you care to sit down?

Veronica No thank you. Have you spoken to the Hartleys?

Morgan Yes, Mrs Nation. Again, not in person, I'm afraid. I'm on my way
there now as a matter of fact. Though Mrs Hartley did report this
morning that your husband left their house last night rather earlier than
was normal, shortly after ten o'clock I believe; something to do with Mr
Hartley feeling unwell.

Veronica Yes, I spoke to Mrs Hartley on the telephone this morning.

Morgan If they can throw any more light on to what exactly happened to
Mr Nation last night, I will, of course, keep you fully informed.

Veronica Thank you.

An awkward pause. Morgan rises

Morgan Constable, would you radio through to the station for me, see if
there's been any developments. Then as soon as Mrs Nation is feeling
herself again we'll be on our way.

Hughes Yes, sir.

Hughes exits

Veronica and Morgan stare at each other for a moment

Veronica (*controlled, but with rising hysteria*) Harry! What the hell are you
doing here? What's going on? This charade is driving me insane!

Morgan Ronnie, darling, you're doing marvellously so far, don't spoil it
now.

He crosses to the doorway to watch for Hughes

Veronica Me *spoil* it? *Me* spoil it? You're not supposed to be here, you're off duty today. You're supposed to be miles away fishing on some stupid river! What do you mean, me spoil it?

Morgan Darling listen, it's not my fault I'm here. What I said before was true, all police leave has been cancelled. They've got every man-jack of us out looking for Gus and those two fishermen. I didn't want to come here, I was *ordered* to come and take your statement!

Veronica Why the hell didn't you warn me?

Morgan I tried, honey, believe me I tried. I phoned and phoned and phoned, but you were out, all day—remember?

Veronica You could've left a message on the tape!

Morgan No thank you! Highly incriminating that would've been. I didn't know when you were coming back. The Station might've sent somebody else down here. He might've snooped around, switched on the answering machine, then goodbye Harry Morgan!

Veronica Oh, I see, it's OK if I'm incriminated as long as you're in the clear, is that it?

Morgan Ronnie, darling, you know I didn't mean that.

Veronica Then why not come alone? Why bring your, your floosie along with you?

Morgan Ronnie don't be silly. It's standard police procedure, when taking a statement, two officers must be present. And she is not my "floosie".

Veronica Well why her? Why not a man?

Morgan Again it is standard procedure. To have a WPC present, if possible, when interviewing a woman.

This is not "strict" Police procedure. He is merely saying it to reassure her. In fact he brought Hughes along as a witness to an "authentic" interview. He was simply looking after number one

Veronica Huh! You make it sound as if you've come here to arrest me. Yes, that's it, isn't it? You're trying to throw all the blame on to me, aren't you? And I suppose she's the little tart who answers your phone for you when you're out of the office. Nice little tête-à-tête you've got going there!

Morgan slaps her across the face. They are both silent for a moment. Then he takes her in his arms

Morgan Darling, darling, darling. I'm sorry. I'm sorry I had to do that. (*He lifts her head, gently*) Now you listen to me; we're almost home, everything's going according to plan, we're on the last lap. Just one more hurdle and we're home and dry. There's only one thing can stop us now, and that's—*ourselves*, you and me, Ronnie. We mustn't fall out, we mustn't suspect each other. I know you've taken the brunt of it, I know it's nerve-racking for you. Just one last effort, mm? Take a deep breath, "stiffen the sinews, summon up the blood!"

Veronica smiles

That's my girl. Now sit down and I'll get you a drink. (*He does so, again looking for Hughes as he passes the doorway*) I must say you had me worried this afternoon. I thought you'd bolted. It looked very suspicious at the time, but I must say your explanation just now was er, "highly convincing". Where *did* you go?

Veronica Harwich?

Morgan Harwich? Why?

Veronica To look for Jeff.

Morgan He'll be on the Continent by now, surely.

Veronica Harry, I don't know where he is. He hasn't telephoned me!

Morgan Are you sure? The tape, while you were out?

Veronica No.

Morgan Perhaps the machine's not working.

Veronica No, the machine's working. There were three calls on it when I got back.

Morgan That does sound odd. (*He hands her a brandy, then stands by doorway looking for Hughes*)

Veronica Harry, he's had three opportunities to phone me. Last night from Harwich, this morning from the Hook, or later in the day when he reached the Valpierre Hotel in Brussels. OK, he was probably pushed for time at Harwich, but he could have phoned from the Hook; that ship docks at seven in the morning.

Morgan And he should've been at the Valpierre hours ago. Did you . . .?

Veronica Yes, I phoned them twice. Once at lunchtime and then again from Harwich this afternoon. The Valpierre haven't seen him. I was about to ring them again when you arrived with that—woman!

Morgan Well, try them again after we've gone.

Veronica But why hasn't he phoned *me*? Harry, I'm worried. If he's had an accident, what do we do?

Morgan If our Jeffrey did meet with an accident somewhere along the way, it could work in our favour.

Veronica How do you mean?

Morgan *If* he had an accident—a fatal one—somewhere on the Continent, then we're rid of him for good, we needn't bother about him ever again.

Veronica Yes, but if he crashed somewhere between here and Harwich then some nosey policeman might begin to wonder why he was driving on the road from Frinton to Harwich and *not* on the road from London to Harwich.

Morgan There's no reason on earth why any investigation should go that far!

Veronica Maybe not, but I couldn't take the risk. That's precisely why I went to Harwich this afternoon. Luckily, there's no sign of an accident anywhere, thank God! But that still doesn't explain where the hell he is or what's happened to him!

The french window curtains remain firmly closed

Morgan There is one thing.

Veronica What?

Morgan The gate, down to the slipway, it was found unlocked this morning, wide open.

Veronica Jeffrey! Oh, God!

Morgan No, don't worry, nobody thought anything of it at the time.

Veronica But he was supposed to lock it and post me the key. If he can make one simple mistake he can make another—and *another*!

Morgan Sh! She's coming back!

Hughes enters

Morgan Well, what kept you?

Hughes Sorry, sir. The Station sergeant would like a word with you on the radio, sir.

Morgan We can do that on the way, Constable. (*He makes to leave*)

Hughes If you'll forgive me, sir, I think you may need to speak to Mrs Nation again, afterwards.

Morgan I see. Would you excuse me a moment, Mrs Nation? (*To Hughes*) Wait here!

Morgan exits

Veronica What's happened? Have they found him?

Hughes I'm afraid I don't know, Mrs Nation. They wouldn't tell me anything.

A pause

May I get you something, ma'am; a brandy perhaps?

Veronica No thanks.

Hughes A cup of tea, coffee?

Veronica No! Thank you.

A pause

Perhaps I will have another brandy after all, if you wouldn't mind?

Hughes Certainly, ma'am.

There is another pause while Hughes fetches the brandy and gives it to Veronica

Morgan enters

Veronica Well?

Morgan I'm afraid it looks like bad news, Mrs Nation. Would you care to sit down?

Veronica Please! (*She remains standing*)

Morgan A man's body has been found down at the Naze, washed up on the beach. There were no personal effects to identify him, but from what is left of his clothing—he appears to have been wearing evening dress.

Veronica I see. Do they want me to identify him?

Morgan No, Mrs Nation. It appears the sea has not been very kind. You would probably find it—impossible to do so. I'm sorry. There was, however, one distinguishing mark, clearly visible, a tattoo on the left forearm, the letters R.O.N.I.K.A.—Ronika. It appears to be some sort of variation of your Christian name, Mrs Nation. Could you confirm that your husband had such a tattoo?

Veronica drops her brandy glass

Veronica No! No! It can't be true!
Morgan Constable!

Hughes makes to approach Veronica

Veronica No, keep away! I don't believe it!
Morgan Constable, more brandy!

Hughes moves to the drinks table

Veronica It's not possible!
Morgan Perhaps if you sat down, Mrs Nation?
Veronica No! (*She feels faint*) Fresh air, give me some fresh air!

Veronica moves to the french windows and opens the curtains. Gus is, of course, standing there wearing Jeffrey's hat and coat. Veronica gasps and steps back

Morgan Gus! *How?*
Gus I'm sorry, my darling, I didn't mean to frighten you like that. Here. (*He sits her down on the chair* L. *He removes his hat and places it on the desk*) Ah! Constable, the very thing, do you mind? (*He takes the brandy from Hughes and hands it to Veronica*) Sip this, darling, you'll feel better. I could do with one of those myself, Constable, if you wouldn't mind. Purely medicinal, of course!

Hughes pours a brandy for Gus

Nice to see you, Harry. Is this an official or a social call?
Morgan Gus, we've had men out looking for you all day. Where have you been?
Gus You tell me!
Morgan You mean, you don't know?
Gus Something like that.
Morgan You, don't—remember?
Gus *Didn't* remember, not at first, anyway. But gradually it's all coming back to me.
Veronica How long had you been there, Gus?
Gus Darling? Are you feeling better?
Veronica How long had you been there? Outside the french windows?
Gus Oh, only a few seconds. I was on my way in, actually. Why do you ask?
Morgan What were you doing out there?
Gus I'd just been across to see Doc König. I had a rather large bump on the back of my head and an excruciating headache. Well, old John König patched me up, no serious damage apparently, and he told me the police have been out looking for me. So I came straight back to the house. Now you're here, you've saved me a phone call.
Morgan But—then who is the man down at the Naze?

Gus Sorry?

Morgan A man's body was washed up on the beach down at the Naze. He was wearing a dinner jacket. They thought it was you.

Gus Oh yes, I think I can explain that.

Morgan You can?

Hughes Perhaps you'd like to start at the beginning, Mr Nation. As far as you can remember. (*She takes notes*)

Gus What a perfectly splendid idea. "As far as I can remember"—ha! Well now, where would you like me to begin?

Hughes Do you remember leaving the Hartley's? They appear to have been the last people to see you.

Gus The Hartley's? Oh yes. I left there rather earlier than usual; John Hartley wasn't feeling quite his old self—too much brandy and soda, I shouldn't wonder. (*He smiles*) Anyway, I walked back along the sea front; the sky was clear to begin with. By the time I reached the railings it had started to rain. I crossed the Greensward, walked up the avenue—it was pelting down by now and the wind was getting up too, so I ran the last few yards to the house and——

Morgan You, actually came back to this house? You remember that?

Gus Oh yes, I remember that—quite clearly!

Veronica Go on.

Gus Well, I came into the hall, took off my wet things and—the phone started to ring. So, I came in here, into this room. I went up to the desk (*he does so*) and I picked up the phone. (*He does so*)

Morgan And then?

Gus Then a blow to the back of my head and—nothing!

Morgan Somebody hit you, knocked you unconscious?

Gus So it would appear.

Hughes Did you see who it was?

Gus I didn't see anything—except a few stars and a lot of bright colours.

Morgan I see, obviously a burglar.

Gus My thoughts exactly.

Veronica And that's all you remember?

Gus Oh no, far from it. That's only the beginning. The next thing I remember, I was being hauled out of the boot of a car by a man I'd never set eyes on before. He was trying to force me into my overcoat of all things, so, I resisted. I pushed him away. It was then I noticed we were down on the lower wall just a few yards from the sea, and the wind, my God, it was a hurricane out there, you couldn't see three feet in front of you.

Hughes (*to Morgan*) It was high tide about that time, sir, eleven fifteen p.m., I believe.

Gus And didn't I know it? Anyway, as I said, I pushed him away and—well, the poor chap looked terrified, as if he'd seen a ghost. I tried to move away from him but he grabbed hold of me and started hitting me. Before long I realized he was trying to lift me up and throw me into the sea. Naturally I hit back; we fought, for some time, I think, and then I hit him in the stomach, he stepped back and—disappeared. Just vanished. It was as if the sea had just swallowed him up. I tried to look for him, but, it was no use.

Hughes You mustn't blame yourself, sir.

Gus The funny thing was, we were both wearing dinner jackets. We must've looked like a couple of battling penguins!

Morgan *A gentleman* burglar, eh? No shortage of them in this town, I'm afraid to say. Well there's no doubt he's the chap we've got down at the Naze. I'm sure we can sort this out without too much fuss.

Gus If he *was* a burglar, Harry, "gentleman" or otherwise, why would he want to kill me? Or even assuming he *did* want to kill me, why drag me all the way down to the sea? Why not kill me here?

Hughes Excuse me, sir, if I might?

Gus Yes, Constable.

Hughes Perhaps this burglar wanted to make it look like an accident, as if you'd been swept out to sea while walking home along the lower wall. That would explain his trying to force you into your overcoat.

Gus It would indeed, Miss . . .?

Hughes Er, Hughes, sir.

Gus Miss Hughes. Very bright young lady you have there, Harry. It would also explain why, when I returned to the car, I found not only my overcoat but also my hat and umbrella lying in the boot. What do you think, Harry?

Morgan Sounds like a, reasonable supposition. Yes, assuming the burglar knew of your movements last night.

Veronica What did you do then, Gus?

Gus Well at the time I had no thoughts of burglars or motives or what-have-you. All I knew was that some stranger had attacked me in my own house and tried to kill me. So, naturally, I thought of Ronnie. What if he'd tried to do the same to her? She was in the house after all. (*He crosses behind her to comfort her*) Probably in her room, I thought. What if she were lying up there unconscious, dead, even. So I jumped into the car, drove up the ramp, through the gate, back up the avenue and . . .

Veronica (*mortified*) You came back, to this house?

Gus No, my darling. That's just it, I didn't. That's where I hit a blank, I'm afraid. I simply don't remember. The next thing I *do* remember is waking up, still in the car, but it was parked in the driveway of number forty-two opposite.

Hughes continues to take notes

(*To Hughes*) That's the Kenton house, they only use it in the summer, but I appear to have parked it deliberately behind the two cedar trees so that I was facing this house. Now the car itself couldn't be seen from the road or from over here, but I could see clearly this house, and everything that went on in it, for that matter.

Morgan What did go on?

Gus (*a moment's pause. He looks at Morgan*) Oh, nothing. It was three a.m. I looked at the dashboard clock. (*He smiles*) The thing is, something had happened. Something I'd seen? Something I heard? Something that stopped me coming back to this house.

Veronica What was it?

Gus (*smiling again*) I didn't know, I couldn't remember, but apparently it was more important than your safety, my darling. Whatever it was it made me change my mind and park the car somewhere where I could spy on this house. (*He shrugs*) Well, at the time I couldn't think straight anyway, I had a splitting headache and I was shivering, it was freezing cold. I found this coat and that hat on the back seat, so I put them on to keep warm. My coat was soaking wet. Then I started searching the car, see if I could find any clues to the identity of my assailant.

Morgan And did you?

Gus Oh yes. I found his passport and a Harwich ferry ticket. (*He takes them both from the coat pocket*) For last night. Obviously his escape route. I don't remember any more, I'm afraid. I guess I passed out again. I woke up some two hours ago.

A pause

Veronica Who was he?

Gus It's rather ironic in a way. If he *had* succeeded in killing me, I can just see the headlines tomorrow morning: "Death of a Nation" (*He chuckles to Veronica*) D. W. Griffiths would have approved of that. Well, in a way, that's exactly what he *did* achieve. (*He opens the passport and reads to Veronica*) His name was *Holland,* Jeffrey *Holland.* (*He chuckles again*)

Morgan Yes, well. (*He is not amused*)

Veronica I think I'll have another drink! (*She crosses to the drinks table*)

Gus Oh, Harry, I'm so sorry, I haven't offered you one. Would you care to?

Morgan No thanks, Gus.

Gus What about the constable. Miss Hughes?

Hughes No thank you, sir.

Gus No? No, I don't think I will, either. Constable, I wonder, would you mind terribly making me a cup of tea. I do so prefer tea to alcohol at moments like these, don't you?

Hughes Well, I ... (*She looks to Morgan for approval*)

Morgan That's all right, Constable, I'll take down any more notes we might need.

Hughes Yes, sir. (*She hands her notebook to Morgan*)

Hughes exits

From now on Morgan does not write anything

Gus Thank you, Harry.

A pause

Veronica At least you're safe, Gus. I'm so glad you're safe.

Gus Yes. And you too, darling.

A pause

Veronica Did you discover what made you change your mind?
Gus Mm? Sorry?
Veronica Why you changed your mind about coming back to the house.
Why you parked the car opposite.
Gus Oh yes, yes, it came to me eventually.

A pause

Morgan Well?
Gus It was the hat!
Veronica The what?
Gus The hat!
Morgan I'm sorry. I don't understand.
Gus It's quite simple, Harry. In the boot of the car was an overcoat, an
umbrella and a hat—all mine.
Morgan So?
Gus When I left the Hartleys last night—you remember I said the sky was
clear—well, I left the hat behind—by mistake, of course. Not unusual, I
don't always wear a hat, very rarely, in fact. So later, when "Mr Holland
the Burglar" presumably saw me walk up the drive, come in the front
door, remove my coat, hang up the umbrella—*No hat!* He could not have
seen me wearing a hat, so why did he put one in the boot of his car? I
assume his plan was to dress me in the overcoat, push me into the sea and
throw the umbrella and hat in after me. But *why*? Why a hat, when he
hadn't seen me wearing one.

A pause. Gus looks at the two of them

Morgan He made a mistake!
Gus No, no. The rest of his plan was meticulous, well thought out, right
down to the get away route, the Harwich ferry. No, he wouldn't make a
mistake like that.
Morgan (*uneasily*) So why did he do it?
Gus Why, indeed? Now let's think back. When he knocked me unconscious
in this room I was wearing only my dinner jacket. So, let us assume that
he watched me approach the house through this window. (*He indicates
window* R) He would've seen my overcoat, yes! And my umbrella, yes. But
it was raining hard and I had the umbrella pulled right down over my
head; so he could not have seen whether I was wearing a hat or not. Now!
I only put the umbrella down once I was safely inside the house, by which
time our Mr Holland was hiding, shall we say, round here. (*He indicates
the recess by the hi-fi*) Ready to attack me should I enter this room.
Wherever he was you can't see the front door from this room anyway. (*He
peers through the doorway*) So, let us say, it was while he was looking out
the window that he assumed, underneath the umbrella, I was wearing a
hat.
Morgan Why would he do that?
Gus Because somebody had told him, that when I left this house earlier I
was indeed wearing a black hat. Now only two people were here when I

left, Harry. One of them was Sally—and as everybody knows she wouldn't, *couldn't* hurt a fly; the other . . .!

Veronica That's preposterous!!

Gus Is it, Ronnie?

Veronica Of course it is! Anyway, I saw you——

She glances at the window R, *realizes her mistake, then stops*

Gus Yes, Ronnie? Go on! You saw me coming up the drive yourself, didn't you? You and boyfriend Jeffrey standing at this window! And naturally you assumed that *underneath* the umbrella I was indeed wearing *a hat*! the same hat I wore when I left here three hours earlier. Then boyfriend Jeffrey knocked me unconscious and carried me out to his car, together with my overcoat, my umbrella and a black trilby hat! There's four or five in the cloakroom, after all! Isn't that how it happened, Veronica?

Veronica You're too damned clever!

Morgan Ronnie, don't!

Veronica Ah, what the hell does it matter; he can't prove anything. OK, Gus, it's all perfectly true. Congratulations! Too bad you sent out the super-efficient Miss Hughes to make tea, she won't be able to take *this* down in writing to be used against me.

Gus looks at Harry

And don't expect any help from Detective Inspector Morgan there; Harry's been in it with me from the start, haven't you Harry?

Morgan (*indicating the notebook*) Sorry, Gus, my pen seems to have run out of ink!

Gus How very inconvenient for you!

Veronica Oh no, Gus. How very inconvenient for *you*!

Morgan You'll never be able to prove this in a million years, you know that don't you? It'll simply be your word against ours. And we shall deny everything most emphatically, I can assure you.

Veronica Such a pity, Harry. It was almost the perfect crime.

Gus Almost! Meticulously laid plot, every move worked out in the finest detail. Oh, you had all the right ingredients, I'll give you that, the only thing is that they all came out in the wrong order. A sort of—anagram of murder, ha! (*He laughs*) Well, the wrong man got killed, didn't he?

Morgan Now don't worry, Ronnie. I shall report this as a simple case of a burglary that went wrong. The burglar thought he'd killed Gus, so he tried to dispose of him in the sea. And if I were you, Gus, I'd go along with that story; you'll make yourself look a fool otherwise.

Gus Oh, I do hate to look a fool, Harry! (*He crosses upstage to the hi-fi equipment*) Veronica, when you arrived home this evening I was already standing behind those curtains. (*He indicates the french windows*)

Veronica You're lying!

Gus You switched on the answering machine; you had, I believe, three calls, including one from Sergeant Webb at the police station?

Veronica looks at Harry in desperation

Then, when you went to the front door to let in Harry and Miss Hughes, I stepped over here, switched on this machine and returned to my hiding place. (*He presses the eject button and removes the cassette tape. He holds it up*) We now have a recording of every word that has been spoken in this room since then.

Morgan My God!

Gus A true confession, in stereophonic sound! I must say, you were much more forthcoming than I thought you'd be, especially when Constable Hughes left you alone.

Veronica That tape will never stand up in court!

Gus As supportive evidence it will. Once they dig up the facts about your affair with Jeffrey Holland ten years ago, that should clinch it.

Veronica How did you . . .?

Gus How did I know? I'm afraid to say that before we married, my darling, I had a private detective dig out your murky past—if there was any—my lawyer's advice, I think it was. I'm glad to say that apart from your romp with Mr Holland it was not so much murky as just slightly "opaque". Until now, that is!

Veronica You bastard!

Gus I rather think my mother would take umbrage at that remark! By the way, Harry, I hope you don't mind, but when you sent Constable Hughes out earlier to radio the police station, I'm afraid I nipped round the back of the house and enlisted her in my cause. She took a bit of persuading, mind you.

We hear the siren of an approaching police car. We see traces of headlights and a flashing blue light through window R

Oh, er, one more thing; she's not out making tea, I'm afraid, she's been summoning the cavalry. I rather suspect they've come to arrest you—both!

Hughes enters

Hughes Would you come along with me now please, Mrs Nation?

Veronica crosses to the doorway, then turns first to look at Harry and then Gus

Veronica Dearest Gus! As I said before, my darling, you're the luckiest man I've ever known!

Gus (*sincerely*) I'm not so sure about that.

Veronica You knew, didn't you?

Gus No, Ronnie. I suspected, I didn't *know* anything!

Veronica Your new book! The notes of your new book, coincidence?

Gus Maybe I was trying to—scare you off.

Veronica (*turning to go*) You should've tried harder!

Veronica exits followed by Hughes

Morgan (*crossing to Gus*) You realize, of course, there's very little on that tape to incriminate *me* in all this.

Gus Oh, Harry, I'm not a vindictive man. But I think there's enough on here to ensure your future as an *ex*-policeman, don't you?

Hughes enters

Morgan How did you know it was me?
Gus I didn't Harry. I didn't know it was you, until you told me. (*He indicates the tape*)

Morgan exits

Hughes Will you be all right, sir?
Gus Yes, fine.

Hughes starts to leave

Oh, and thank you, Constable, for all your help.
Hughes My pleasure, sir. I haven't had so much excitement for years!

Hughes exits

Gus crosses to the window R. *He is exhausted and thoroughly dejected by his experience. Car doors are heard to slam, the blue police light is extinguished and the car headlights disappear as the car drives off. All is quiet*

Sally enters from the french windows with some cardboard files

Sally Ah, Mr Nation, I'm awfully glad I've caught you in. I've done all your typing bang-up-to-date. Here we are.

She drops the pile of cardboard files on the desk

And you'll never guess what, I've solved that thing of yours, that riddle, whatchamacallit? Nanagram, you remember? Wilhelm Paprio, that private detective chappie? Well, the only other name I could get out of it was Philip Marlowe. Now George has never heard of him, but I'm certain I've seen him in one of them old "Bogey" films. Am I right, sir?
Gus Spot on, Sally.
Sally I knew it! I knew I'd seen him somewhere. Humphrey Bogart and Lauren Bacall, I think it was, but I can't remember what it was called. Er, where's Mrs Nation, sir? She'll be tickled pink I've done it.
Gus (*wearily*) *The Big Sleep.*
Sally Sorry? What was that, sir?
Gus *The Big Sleep*, Sally.
Sally Oh, I see. (*She doesn't*) Mrs Nation gone for a rest then, has she, sir?
Gus You could say that, Sally, you could say that!
Sally Oh, well. Eh! You'll never guess what, sir! (*She giggles*) What's my name?
Gus Mm?
Sally Oh, never mind. My name's Sally Dure, right? D.U.R.E.?
Gus (*smiling*) Yes, Sally.
Sally And George, my old man, is George Dure. Or if you like, Mr Dure. Now, what is a nanagram of Mr Dure? Abbreviated mister, of course.

Gus I've no idea, Sally. Do tell me!

Sally (*mischievously*) *Murder*. *Mr Dure* is a ṇanagram of *Murder*! (*She laughs*) Isn't that funny?

Gus (*with no enthusiasm*) That's very clever, Sally. "An Anagram of Murder", that'd make a splendid title for a play. Remind me to write it one day, will you?

Gus exits

CURTAIN

FURNITURE AND PROPERTY LIST

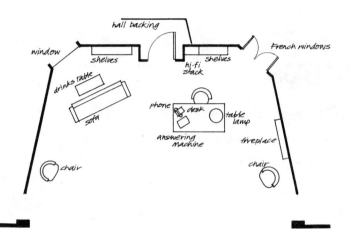

ACT I

SCENE 1

On stage: Three upright chairs
Sofa
Drinks table. *On it:* several bottles and glasses (including a bottle of bourbon), ice, mixers etc
Desk with drawers. *On it:* table lamp, answering machine, telephone, pens. *In drawers:* buff files, pack of cards, string, envelopes, stamps, key
Hi-fi stack, including tuner, amplifier, cassette player and record deck
Two areas of shelving. *On them:* records, tapes, books. Statuette on shelving R
Clock on mantlepiece
Curtains at both windows
Carpet
Dressing as desired

Off stage: TV magazines **(Veronica)**
Bow tie **(Gus)**

Overcoat, hat, umbrella **(Gus)**
Shopping bag **(Sally)**

Personal: **Veronica:** wristwatch

SCENE 2

Personal: **Jeffrey:** distinctive hat, sheepskin coat
Sally: key

ACT II
SCENE 1

No further props

SCENE 2

Set: Passport and ferry ticket in Jeffrey's coat pocket

Off stage: Cardboard files **(Sally)**

Personal: **Hughes:** notebook and pen

LIGHTING PLOT

A study/drawing room. Practical fittings required: table lamp

ACT I, SCENE 1

To open: Darkness

Cue 1	**Recorded voice:** "... I tell you, nothing at all." *Light comes on in hall*	(Page 1)
Cue 2	**Veronica** switches on main light *Snap on main lighting*	(Page 1)
Cue 3	**Gus** switches on table lamp *Snap on table lamp*	(Page 2)

ACT I, SCENE 2

To open: All lights on

Cue 4	**Veronica** turns off main light *Snap off main light, leaving hall and table lamp*	(Page 20)

ACT II, SCENE 1

To open: As close of Act I

Cue 5	**Veronica:** "*Damn!*" *Car headlights seen through window* R. *Then extinguish*	(Page 26)
Cue 6	As car starts again *Headlights seen through window*	(Page 26)
Cue 7	When ready *Lights move off as car draws away*	(Page 27)

ACT II, Scene 2

To open: Dusk. No lights on

Cue 8	Car approaches *Headlights seen through window* R. *Then extinguish*	(Page 27)
Cue 9	As hall door opens *Hall light goes on*	(Page 27)
Cue 10	**Veronica** switches on lamp *Snap on lamp*	(Page 27)
Cue 11	As car approaches *Headlights seen through window* R	(Page 28)

Cue 12   **Veronica** switches on main light   (Page 28)
            Snap on main light

Cue 13   **Gus:** "... bit of persuading, mind you."   (Page 40)
            *Flashing blue light of police car and headlights through the
            window*

Cue 14   **Gus** goes to window   (Page 41)
            Blue light extinguished. Headlights go as car drives away

EFFECTS PLOT

ACT I

Cue 1   As Curtain rises   (Page 1)
           Radio recording as script. Cut when Veronica switches it off

Cue 2   As **Veronica** opens french windows   (Page 6)
           Wind howling in trees

Cue 3   **Veronica:** "Perfect!"   (Page 6)
           Clock chimes three-quarters

Cue 4   **Gus:** "... no, that wouldn't work."   (Page 7)
           Telephone rings

Cue 5   As **Veronica** goes to drinks table   (Page 9)
           Front door closes

Cue 6   As **Veronica** goes to doorway   (Page 15)
           Key heard in front door

Cue 7   As **Jeffrey** goes to exit   (Page 18)
           Telephone rings

Cue 8   When ready   (Page 18)
           Door opens and closes in hall

Cue 9   As Jeffrey picks up statuette   (Page 21)
           Key heard in front door, then door closes

Cue 10   **Veronica:** "Wait, I think he's ..."   (Page 21)
           Door opens and closes

Cue 11   **Jeffrey:** "OK."   (Page 21)
           Phone rings

ACT II

Cue 12   **Veronica:** "*Damn.*"   (Page 26)
           Car approaches

Cue 13   **Veronica** and **Jeffrey** exit   (Page 26)
           Front door opens. Car doors open and close. Car engine heard

Cue 14   When ready   (Page 27)
           Phone rings. Car moves off. Front door closes

Cue 15   At beginning of Scene 2   (Page 27)
           Car approaches and stops. Car door opens and closes. Front door
           opens and closes

Cue 16   **Veronica** switches on answering machine   **(Page 27)**
            Recording played as text

Cue 17   **Veronica** switches off tape   **(Page 28)**
            Snap off tape

Cue 18   **Veronica** is about to dial on phone   **(Page 28)**
            Car approaches

Cue 19   **Gus:** ". . . bit of persuading, mind you."   **(Page 40)**
            Police car siren. Cut when car arrives

Cue 20   **Gus** goes to window   **(Page 41)**
            Car door slams. Car drives off

MADE AND PRINTED IN GREAT BRITAIN BY
LATIMER TREND & COMPANY LTD PLYMOUTH
MADE IN ENGLAND